JOHN ADAMS

The Presidents of the United States

George Washington
1789–1797

John Adams
1797–1801

Thomas Jefferson
1801–1809

James Madison
1809–1817

James Monroe
1817–1825

John Quincy Adams
1825–1829

Andrew Jackson
1829–1837

Martin Van Buren
1837–1841

William Henry Harrison
1841

John Tyler
1841–1845

James Polk
1845–1849

Zachary Taylor
1849–1850

Millard Fillmore
1850–1853

Franklin Pierce
1853–1857

James Buchanan
1857–1861

Abraham Lincoln
1861–1865

Andrew Johnson
1865–1869

Ulysses S. Grant
1869–1877

Rutherford B. Hayes
1877–1881

James Garfield
1881

Chester Arthur
1881–1885

Grover Cleveland
1885–1889

Benjamin Harrison
1889–1893

Grover Cleveland
1893–1897

William McKinley
1897–1901

Theodore Roosevelt
1901–1909

William H. Taft
1909–1913

Woodrow Wilson
1913–1921

Warren Harding
1921–1923

Calvin Coolidge
1923–1929

Herbert Hoover
1929–1933

Franklin D. Roosevelt
1933–1945

Harry Truman
1945–1953

Dwight Eisenhower
1953–1961

John F. Kennedy
1961–1963

Lyndon Johnson
1963–1969

Richard Nixon
1969–1974

Gerald Ford
1974–1977

Jimmy Carter
1977–1981

Ronald Reagan
1981–1989

George H. W. Bush
1989–1993

William J. Clinton
1993–2001

George W. Bush
2001–2009

ts and Their Times

JOHN ADAMS
WIL MARA

mc Marshall Cavendish
Benchmark
New York

Marshall Cavendish Benchmark
99 White Plains Road
Tarrytown, New York 10591-5502
www.marshallcavendish.us

Library of Congress Cataloging-in-Publication Data

Mara, Wil.
John Adams / by Wil Mara.
p. cm. —(Presidents and their times)
Summary: "Provides comprehensive information on President John Adams and places
him within his historical and cultural context. Also explored are the formative events of
his times and how he responded"—Provided by publisher.
Includes bibliographical references and index.
ISBN 978-0-7614-2840-4
1. Adams, John, 1735–1826—Juvenile literature. 2. Presidents—United States—Biography—
Juvenile literature. 3. United States—History—Revolution, 1775–1783—Juvenile literature.
4. United States—Politics and government—1775–1783—Juvenile literature. 5. United States—
Politics and government—1783–1809—Juvenile literature. I. Title.
E322.M34 2008
973.44092—dc22
[B]2007023410

Editor: Christine Florie
Publisher: Michelle Bisson
Art Director: Anahid Hamparian
Series Designer: Alex Ferrari

Photo research by Connie Gardner

Cover photo by Portrait of John Adams (oil on canvas) by Gilbert Stuart (1755–1822)
(after) c Musee Franco Americane, Bleran court, Chauny, France/The Bridgeman Art
Library Nationality/copyright status: American/out of copyright.

The photographs in this book are used by permission and through the courtesy of: *The Bridgeman
Art Library:* John Adams (b & w photo of engraving) by Houston, H. (19th c.)/Private Collection, 6;
Private Collection/Peter Newark American Pictures, 10; State Historical Society of Wisconsin, Madison,
USA, 33; Celebration of the Repeal of the Stamp Act, from the Boston Gazette, 19th May, 1766
(newsprint) by American School (18th century) c America Antiquarian Society, Worcester, Massachusetts,
USA, 38; First in War. First in Peace and First in the hearts of his Countrymen (litho) by American School
(19th century) c Collection of the New York Historical Society, USA, 69; John Adams (1735–1826).
1823 (oil on canvas) by Gilbert Stuart (1755–1828) c Museum of Fine Arts, Boston, Massachusetts,
USA/Bequest of Charles Francis Adams, 97, 101 (R); *Corbis:* Bettmann, 11, 14, 16, 29, 43, 46, 78, 100 (L);
Poodles Rock, 49; Profiles in History, 95; *Getty Images:* Hulton Archive, 18, 27; Time and Life Pictures, 66;
Alamy: North Wind Pictures Archive, 25; *North Wind Pictures Archives:* 19, 35, 41, 50, 56; *The Granger
Collection:* 3, 23, 36, 45, 53, 58, 60, 63, 72, 75, 81, 83, 85, 87, 90, 93, 99, 101 (L), 100 (R).

Printed in Malaysia
1 3 5 6 4 2

CONTENTS

John Adams holds a stately place among the nation's founding fathers who supported the separation of the American colonies from England and, ultimately, was elected the second president of the United States.

A President is Born

The House Chamber of Philadelphia's Congress Hall filled with excitement, nervousness, anticipation, and fear. All in attendance knew they were about to witness an important moment in the history of their young nation. They were senators and representatives, cabinet secretaries and Supreme Court justices—the leaders of the American people and the most brilliant minds of their time. The date was March 4, 1797.

The main door opened shortly before noon, and in walked the man most of them considered the first true American hero, President George Washington. Greeted with thunderous applause, he kept his usual calm. He went past the rows of tables and chairs that formed a half circle in the center of the room and made his way to a raised platform. More cheering came with the arrival of the tall and handsome Thomas Jefferson, who seemed even taller in his long coat. This was another hero, one who had devoted his best ideas and energies to ensuring the freedom of his fellow citizens, most notably as the author of the document that changed the course of the world, the Declaration of Independence.

Finally, John Adams appeared. The crowd erupted in cheers once again. Unlike Washington and Jefferson, Adams was a short, roundish man, hardly the image of a heroic figure. Yet he was regarded in exactly that way. Even those who disagreed with his principles and beliefs—and there were many in the room—could not deny that he had played an invaluable role in leading the country through one of its darkest and most difficult periods.

Adams felt little happiness on this day thus far. His beloved wife and family were unable to attend. He also had slept poorly the night before, fearing he would be too nervous to make it through the ceremony.

Adams found his confidence as the audience became caught up in the spirit of the occasion. He strode to the front of the room, took the oath of office, then gave his inaugural address. He spoke of his respect for the American people and the developing American way of life. He believed in the governmental system of his new nation—one that he helped create. He took time to thank Washington for his superb service and leadership. And he told everyone present that he was determined to build a government that would devote itself to the needs of *all* the people, not just those with power or money. It was a meaningful and stirring speech, and it brought tears to the eyes of some. Even Adams himself was surprised by the force with which it was delivered. When he was through, the country had its new leader—one who was highly regarded, even among his enemies, for his honesty and his belief in doing what was right.

John Adams had met and conquered many great challenges before this day, and he knew more would come in the years ahead. But he was dedicated to doing whatever it took to build a strong and stable society. With so many years of hard work behind him, he was ready to be the president of the United States.

BIRTH

John Adams was born in Braintree, Massachusetts, on October 30, 1735 (although it was October 19 according to the calendar in use at that time). He was the oldest of three brothers; Peter and Elihu were the others.

John's father, also named John, was a farmer and a **deacon**. His farmland had belonged to the Adamses for over a century. John Senior was a kind and decent man who believed in hard work, doing things right, and the importance of home and family. His son idolized and adored him, once writing in a letter that he was "the honestest man" that he ever knew. His father also had a great love of his country, which he obviously passed down to his son.

John's mother, Susanna Boylston, came from a family of respected physicians. Because she came from an important family, some people in Braintree may have felt that her marriage to the elder John Adams—whose ancestors had never been to college and spent their lives working in fields all day—was a mismatch. But the Adamses were a proud group, and they, too, were well respected. By all accounts, John held the same affection for his mother as he did his father. Susanna was a strong-minded woman with plenty of energy and, at times, a wild temper. Young John inherited these characteristics from her, and they played a key role in forming the man he would eventually become.

CHILDHOOD

Adams had a happy and fulfilling childhood. At times, in fact, it seemed almost dreamlike. The town of Braintree had much to offer an adventurous little boy—there were gentle hills, sturdy forests, sun-dappled streams and creeks, and long stretches of beachfront that hugged the edges of nearby bays and rivers. Adams spent hours hiking, fishing, and hunting as he explored the natural beauties of his world. He learned to love the outdoors, and he would carry this love into adulthood.

The house in which he was born and raised was similar in character to his family—simple, yet solid and dignified. It had been built in the late 1600s and had five rooms; three downstairs and two upstairs. It also had two chimneys. In spite of this, it could still become very cold during the brutal New England winters, forcing the family to wear blankets or coats indoors. When someone had to go to the bathroom, he or she had to go outside—regardless of how cold or hot it was—because the house

John Adams's birthplace is the oldest presidential birthplace in the United States. He was born in the home on the right.

P
***********2926

John Adams /
jnfb
33305216588586

Expires 02/15/24

Thu

02/05/24 12:33PM

John Adams's childhood was a happy one. He enjoyed many different outdoor activities.

didn't have any indoor plumbing. Similarly, when the family wanted fresh water, they had to lower a bucket into a well that was also outside.

It wasn't always easy living in such a house but, by all accounts, the Adamses were a happy family. They often had houseguests—friends and relatives—and played games or read books for fun. John and his brothers were allowed to speak their minds on almost any subject, which was unusual at a time when children were often told not to say anything unless an adult said something to them first. They would discuss everything from science and math to religion and politics. John's parents also taught their children the importance of being humble, truthful, and thrifty.

The Adams family, therefore, was very similar to most others in New England. Most eighteenth-century New Englanders believed the best way to live your life was to work hard, expect few rewards, and behave in a way that was honorable in the

LEARNING LESSONS

Young John, like anyone else, had his share of bad habits. One was his famous stubbornness, and there is one famous story about it.

John's father was determined to send his three sons to college, as he hoped they would not have to endure the hardships of a farmer's life. So he urged them to do their very best in school. But one day, while frustrated with his schooling, young John told his father that he wanted to become a farmer after all. The elder Adams pretended to be pleased and told his son that he could start his farming career immediately by helping him remove a thick layer of dead grass and leaves by a creek on their property. John happily agreed. He soon discovered the work to be backbreakingly hard. After the first day, he still claimed a love for farmwork. After the second day, however, John finally admitted he'd made a mistake—and rather than face a lifetime of punishing physical labor, he hurried back to his books.

eyes of God. Purity of mind and soul were prized above all else—certainly above the desire for material things and luxuries.

School Days

Adams learned how to read, as did many youngsters of his time, at home. After that he took basic lessons in the house of a woman in his neighborhood, who also taught other local children. Then young John began going to a proper schoolhouse, but he soon discovered that he didn't like the teacher, and his work began to suffer. He lost his enthusiasm for learning, and his performance suffered. His father, rather than becoming angry with him, took him out of this school and enrolled him in another. John liked his new teacher much better, and he soon began doing well again. He was a good student, curious about many things. And due to his excellent grades and positive attitude, he was eventually admitted to attend, starting in 1751, the finest college in the colony—Harvard College, roughly 13 miles away in the Massachusetts town of Cambridge. So proud of his son's achievement and his bright future, his father sold some of his land to help pay the tuition.

Among the happiest days of John Adams's life were those he spent at Harvard. He studied many subjects, but he liked math and science best. He also discovered a love of reading that would stay with him for the rest of his life. Harvard could be very strict, expecting its students to behave themselves at all times, even when they weren't in class. They had to get up early, go to the campus church for morning prayers, then to their classrooms, and then back to the church for end-of-day prayers before dinnertime. Adams didn't seem to mind and in fact appeared to enjoy

Adams attended Harvard College from 1751–1755.

the orderliness of it. He also made many friends, some of whom he kept in touch with for years after graduation.

It is interesting to note that Adams's father initially hoped his son would study religion at Harvard and eventually become a minister. And at first he did his best to comply with his father's wishes. But it soon became apparent that he didn't really have all the talents necessary for such a profession. For example, his public-speaking skills were considered average at best.

Then one of his instructors suggested that he might make a better lawyer. Adams soon discovered that he liked the idea of this occupation, and he was pleased to find that his father was not disappointed by the change in focus. When Adams graduated, in 1755, his plans for a life as a minister were long gone. It's hard not to wonder how the future of America would have been different if he'd stuck with his father's original plan. But just as he had changed, so the course of his country was changing—in the form of a war that started thousands of miles away but eventually landed on Adams's doorstep.

Old World Meets New

By the mid-1400s, nations within Europe and Asia were developing advanced technologies, forming powerful governments, and amassing tremendous wealth. In order for people to conduct business, they had to travel to other regions. The pathways that allowed this travel, called trade routes, were usually on land, reached by horse or on foot. Unfortunately for the businessmen of Europe, most trade routes were controlled by Arabs, making it very difficult and expensive for them to reach their Asian neighbors. As a result the Europeans decided to take to the sea in search of new trade routes—those that could be traveled on the world's waterways.

In the year 1492, on Spain's behalf, the explorer Christopher Columbus began searching for a water passage to Asia. Roughly two months later, he sailed into a group of islands. Some historians believe this was the island of San Salvador in the Bahamas.

It didn't take long for the rulers of Europe to realize that not only had they stumbled upon a whole new world (which would eventually, in fact, come to be known as the New World) but that it was also a tremendous source of many valuable goods they

While searching for new trade routes for Spain, Christopher Columbus landed on San Salvador in 1492.

could sell and trade back home—precious metals, various agricultural products, and so on.

ENGLAND VERSUS FRANCE

France sent people to colonize North America before England did, and these French colonists built most of their early communities in two main areas—along the St. Lawrence River (the main waterway that runs north of the present-day New England states and south of Quebec and Ontario in Canada) and in islands in the Caribbean on which they could harvest sugar, which was a prized agricultural item at the time. France also sent explorers farther inland to scout other areas in which future colonists might live. At that time the French concentrated mostly on acquiring the fur pelts of beavers, raccoons, and foxes, as they were in great demand back in their native country.

Then the English came. By the mid-1500s England was involved in a religious war within its own borders. Also, England was becoming too crowded. Open land was becoming scarce, and it was hard simply to find places to live. So these two factors drove thousands of native English people to America.

With so many different European countries represented in the colonies, fights broke out over which nation would have the greatest control in the New World. The French and the English became the leading competitors for this prize.

Between the years 1689 and 1763 England and France engaged in four separate wars. The first three were relatively small, and in North America they focused on the same struggle for power and domination in the New World. Both sides wanted control of the fur trade, the sugar trade, and anything else that

Settlers from England began arriving in North America in the 1500s and established their first permanent settlement in Jamestown, Virginia in 1607.

gave them an edge. Both sides used not only the military services of their home nations but also their own colonists as well as Native Americans. Even the people who had been living in North America long before the first Europeans arrived eventually had to choose sides in the fighting.

Very little changed as a result of these three wars. England did manage to capture and claim some territory from the French and Spanish (and smaller colonies, like those held by the Dutch, lost a tremendous amount of influence in the area). But England's

English trade was disrupted by the Spanish, who captured English ships as they carried supplies to the North American colonies.

quest for complete power was far from over. Outside of North America, England was also battling France and Spain on other fronts. For example, Spain tried to stop English ships from coming and going to the English colonies, thereby causing great harm to Britain's overseas trade efforts.

Meanwhile, John Adams's days at his beloved Harvard were coming to an end. He loved the experience and was saddened by the thought of putting it behind him. He had met many new people, including some who would leave a lifelong impression. He had discovered his true passion—law—plus further interests in mathematics and science. He had been exposed to more new and fascinating books than he could have dared to imagine—and, like a child in a candy shop, he devoured them all. And he had behaved himself, earning only one blemish on his record—he once returned late from a vacation. Otherwise, he was an exemplary and hardworking student.

Elsewhere in the world, however, not everything was quite as rosy. As Adams was graduating, in 1755, the last of the four wars between the great European powers was starting to boil. This would be the final battle to decide who would control the New World. And while young Adams was trying to decide his future, destiny was forming its own set of plans for him.

A MAN AND HIS COUNTRY

John Adams returned to his hometown of Braintree after graduating from Harvard. But he did not remain there long; he soon found work roughly 60 miles away, in the town of Worcester. There he became a teacher in a small schoolhouse. He had about a dozen students, both boys and girls, and he did his best to teach them the basics of language, math, science, and so on. He was a good instructor who believed in motivating his students through encouragement rather than punishment. But although he enjoyed being around them and watching their minds develop, he was bored by the job itself. It didn't seem to offer much of a future, and the pay was awful (so low, in fact, that he couldn't even afford his own home—he had to live with others). He often found his attention wandering as he daydreamed of the more important things he might do with his life. This was a period of soul-searching for Adams. He tried to improve his personality, break bad habits, and search for his true calling in life.

At the time the only other professions worth considering were medicine, ministry, or law. Adams did, in fact, think for a short time that he might go into medicine and become a doctor. This, no doubt, would have pleased his mother's family, which had many noted doctors already. But he eventually decided to become a lawyer. There were several lawyers he had heard and seen in local courtrooms, and their performances dazzled him. Also, since Adams had such strong moral beliefs, he saw the law as an opportunity to right wrongs and fight for people who didn't have the means to fight for them-selves. The legal profession, overall, was not considered very respectable, but Adams knew that was largely because some of the people who were lawyers were not respectable. Adams knew the law itself, and with its awesome power at his com-mand, he could do a lot of good.

Back in those days, there were no law schools—you didn't simply go to a school, get your degree, and become a lawyer. Instead, you had to study under someone who was already a lawyer. You also had to pay that person a fee for this privilege. Adams eventually found a man who let him do that. In August of 1756 he agreed to pay a Worcester lawyer by the name of James Putnam the sum of $100 (a tremendous amount at the time), and in return Adams would study law under Putnam's guidance for two years.

By all accounts, those two years were mostly happy ones for Adams, still a young man. He continued teaching his beloved schoolchildren during the day and studied under Putnam in his off hours. Also during this time the war with the French and their allies was in full swing. Adams would see England's royal troops all over Worcester. It is worth noting that Adams did not feel any resentment toward them at this point and, in fact, even felt somewhat proud to be a British citizen. Like other colonists, he was angered by the aggression of the French and wanted to see his army win the war and gain full control of America. There was no way he could have known how differently he would feel about Mother England in the years ahead. At this stage in his life he was simply concentrating on finding his own place in the world.

Adams finished his studies with Putnam in the fall of 1758 and returned to Braintree. With his law training behind him, he

English troops were positioned in Massachusetts during England's fight for North American territory in the mid-1700s.

had to focus on passing the bar exam—the test that all law students must take before being able to actually work as lawyers. But he also wanted to spend some time enjoying his hometown, his family, and his friends again. Between his Harvard years and his teaching/law training in Worcester, he hadn't been able to do so in almost eight years. He even tried his hand at some farmwork—the type of grueling labor that drove him back to his schoolbooks as a boy. But this time he found himself liking it. Indeed, he had grown up and left his boyhood behind in so many ways. He passed the bar exam and was ready to work in his exciting new career.

BAD TIMES

Unfortunately, Adams's enthusiasm was temporarily dampened when he lost his very first case after opening his own law office. His client was a farmer who'd lost some crops when a few horses belonging to a neighbor trampled them after escaping from the neighbor's property. While the neighbor did manage to get the horses out of the man's fields, the farmer wanted to be repaid for the crops that had been lost. Adams believed his client was right, and he argued the case well. But he made some mistakes in the case's paperwork, and the judge ruled in favor of the neighbor. The farmer was extremely angry with Adams, and Adams didn't blame him. For all his extensive legal training, he was no expert in fine points like the correct way to write up legal papers.

He was deeply disappointed with himself, but he vowed never to make such foolish mistakes again. He pushed himself harder than ever, closely studying the lawyers he admired as they worked their magic in court. He tried to figure out how and why they did the things they did, tried to understand the thoughts and

By studying other lawyers in the courtroom, John Adams improved his own skills.

principles that guided them. In time his skills improved, and he began gaining confidence in himself. He believed that he could, in spite of his earlier failure, still be a great lawyer. But then he suffered another blow—a personal one that would scar him forever.

John's beloved father died in late May of 1761, the victim of influenza. This is a viral disease that attacks the chest and lungs, causing the victim difficulty in breathing and general weakness. Although usually treatable today, it was often deadly in Adams's time and attacked many people at once, since it spreads quickly. John

Senior was seventy years old at the time of his death, and more than a dozen others in Braintree perished as well. John's mother also contracted the illness, but she survived.

Crushed by the loss, Adams became more determined than ever to make something of himself and his legal career. In his will John Senior had left John a house (which stood next to the one in which the younger John was raised) and 40 acres of land. Adams took great pride in this new property, building a small addition onto the home and using it as the first office for his law practice. With his family's strong local reputation and Adams's slowly building his own reputation as a man of decency and honor, his practice was soon thriving. He got to know and befriend not only other lawyers but also several important judges and politicians. He enjoyed his profession more than ever, and he was becoming a fairly important man around town.

The Lawyer Takes a Wife

The other major development in Adams's life during this period was his marriage to Abigail Smith in 1764. He'd first met Smith in 1759 through a group of friends. She was a small and pretty girl with brown hair and brown eyes. She was remarkably well educated for someone who had been taught at home and had never been inside a formal school. Like Adams, she loved to read, and she had a cheerful nature that warmed Adams's heart. This provided a balance to his habit of sometimes being too harsh and negative. Smith was also one of the few people who knew how to criticize Adams without upsetting him. She saw and admired the goodness in him that others often missed or, at the very least, misunderstood.

Abigail Smith married John Adams in 1764.

The Marriage that Never Was

John Adams almost married someone other than Abigail Smith. There was a young woman in his hometown of Braintree named Hannah Quincy, the daughter of the respected and wealthy Josiah Quincy. She was easygoing, funny, and somewhat flirty—and Adams, along with several of his friends, was interested in her. Adams worked hard for her affections, taking long walks with her around Braintree. He even read a book about marriage written by the great Benjamin Franklin, with whom he would one day be friends. Then one night Adams decided to ask Hannah to marry him—but one of his friends, along with one of Hannah's cousins, burst into the room and disrupted him before he could say anything. He never got another chance, and Hannah Quincy eventually married someone else.

The couple was married in the autumn of 1764 and moved into Adams's home in Braintree. Abigail went to work as the perfect New England housewife, sewing the clothes, feeding the animals, and cooking the meals. She preferred doing all of this on her own and was quite good at it. In July of the following year she bore their first child—also named Abigail but nicknamed Nabby. Two years later came another child, a son whom they named John Quincy. Adams was happier than he had ever been, with a wonderful wife, two beautiful children, and a busy career. It seemed as if his life couldn't get any fuller. But it would.

By the late 1760s, Adams was enjoying a content life with a growing career and family.

The Beginnings of a War

During those years when Adams was busy getting his law career off the ground, getting married, and starting a family, the final conflict developed between France and England for control of North America. The French and Indian War began, for the most part, with a series of small but important battles in and around the Ohio River. This area, known as the Ohio River Valley, was crucial to both sides, as it meant gaining more land, more transportation routes, and a greater involvement in important businesses like the fur trade.

At the start of the war, the Ohio River Valley was occupied and controlled by a collection of Native-American tribes known as the Iroquois Confederacy. The British and the French both wanted to change this, because they knew the eventual control of the entire continent was dependent on control of this region. Eventually, the English did begin seeping into the area, trying to make friends with the Iroquois. The French, fearing that the English were now gaining too much ground, began building military forts in the valley, particularly along the Allegheny River, in Pennsylvania. In response, the governor of Virginia, Robert Dinwiddie, asked for help from a promising young lieutenant colonel named George Washington. He instructed Washington to deliver a message to the French saying, essentially, to get out of the area and go back to Canada. The French, of course, ignored these demands. So less than a year later, Dinwiddie ordered the construction of a British fort in a key location in the area—the meeting point of the Allegheny and Monongahela rivers.

THE BATTLE OF THE GREAT MEADOWS

Now the French became even more worried. They decided that the only way to handle the situation was through military force. A group of French soldiers overran the British fort, sent Washington and his men back to Virginia, and built their own fort on the site—Fort Duquesne. Afterward, they began thinking of the Ohio River Valley as their own. Not to be outdone, the British sent another group of their own soldiers—again under the command of George Washington—back to the same area. Washington's orders this time were to clear a road through the forest so that more troops could get into the region.

Once this road was completed, Washington and some of his men—about forty in total—came across a group of French soldiers, and a battle ensued. Washington's men won this brief battle. Afterward, they built a small fort in a nearby clearing and named it Fort Necessity. It was probably a very simple structure—a tiny storehouse and sleeping quarters surrounded by a circular stockade fence. It was built crudely and without much attention to detail. Then again, it was meant to be only temporary; a place for men to rest, eat, and be protected while they continued clearing the woodland road to the Ohio River. Chances are it would have been abandoned shortly thereafter and never used again. But on July 3, 1754, the fort was attacked by over seven hundred troops—mostly French soldiers, but also some Native Americans who had sided with them—and the battle ended with Washington's suffering heavy losses. Washington was forced to surrender, and by the next day he and his remaining soldiers were once again sent back to Virginia. The

French then burned Fort Necessity to the ground. Most historians consider this battle—known as the Battle of the Great Meadows—to be the true start of the French and Indian War.

The rulers of Great Britain were against the idea of fighting yet another war with France and its allies. The last three, although relatively small, had caused the nation great financial hardship, and it was deeply in debt. The last thing the rulers wanted to do was pour money into a long and expensive crusade. In the end, the British government sent small numbers of troops across the Atlantic Ocean, hoping that would be enough and that the problem would be solved quickly and easily.

Around the same time, leaders from seven of the British colonies in North America got together to make plans for whatever battles might occur. One of the smartest things they did was to meet with the leaders of the Iroquois Confederacy to see if the Iroquois would consider fighting with them against the French. Since the Confederacy had many who knew the area well, its help would make an enormous difference. In return, the British gave the Iroquois men who agreed to help everything from blankets and food to guns and ammunition.

THE FRENCH TAKE THE LEAD—AT FIRST

The French took an early lead in the war. During one of the first battles, in 1755, a British general named Edward Braddock, along with about 1,500 of his soldiers, tried to take control of France's Fort Duquesne. Braddock had roughly one-third more troops than the French, so he seemed to have an advantage. But the French and their Native-American allies waged a better fight and, in the end, the British were forced to retreat. Braddock suffered a serious wound that killed him a few days

British general Edward Braddock and his troops battled the French and their Native-American allies at Fort Duquesne.

later, and several hundred men were lost. In 1756 the French went on to capture an important British fort in New York known as Fort Oswego, which protected a busy trading post. They also destroyed Britain's Fort William Henry, also in New York, in 1757.

Things then began to change in Britain's favor. In June of 1757 a man named William Pitt became Britain's prime minister. Pitt was a firm supporter of the war against France, and he persuaded his government to send more troops, guns, ammunition, and other supplies to North America. His timing was also perfect—due to the few victories that the French did manage to score in the early stages of the war, France seriously lessened its army presence.

The British took advantage of this, driving French forces out of numerous forts and other settlements and capturing and claiming land all along the Ohio Valley and into Canada. From 1757 to 1758 Pitt instructed the British generals to focus most of their efforts in Canada, and he sent thousands of troops to finish the job. By 1760 most of the fighting was over. In September, with nothing left under their control but the city of Montreal, the French surrendered.

RESULTS OF THE WAR—BOTH GOOD AND BAD

As a result of the French and Indian War the royal government of Britain got what it wanted—full control of North America. It also gained many other French possessions around the world, including trading posts in West Africa, India, and several small islands. This, of course, left a bitter taste in France's mouth—one that would drive France to play a key role in the relationship between Britain and its American colonists in the years ahead.

And for Great Britain the victory wasn't without problems, either—the financial struggles it had before the war were now much worse. The nation was deeper in debt than ever, and Britain's leaders had to figure out a way to pay it. They eventually decided to take money from the colonists in the form of new taxes. The British government already had some taxes in place—for example, every time the colonists received shipments of sugar or molasses from overseas, they had to pay the British government a small amount of money.

The Stamp Act of 1765

One of the first major steps the British Parliament took toward taxing the colonists was to pass the **Stamp Act** in 1765. This required that all paper items—such as mortgages, newspapers, and even playing cards—carry an official stamp of the British government. It also meant that the colonists would have to pay a tax for using these items. Without the stamp the papers would be considered invalid, which would cause enormous problems. The colonists, unsurprisingly, took great offense at the Stamp Act. Many of them refused to honor it, ignoring it altogether.

> S T A M P · O F F I C E,
> *Lincoln's-Inn,* 1765.
>
> A
>
> # T A B L E
>
> **Of the Prices of Parchment and Paper for the Service of *America.***
>
> Parchment.   Paper.
>
> Skins 18 Inch. by 13, at Fourpence   Horn at Seven-pence
>   22 —— by 16, at Six-pence   Fools Cap at Nine-pence
>   26 —— by 20, at Eight-pence each. D° with printed Notices at
>   28 —— by 23, at Ten-pence   for Indentures   1 s.
>   31 —— by 26, at Thirteen-pence.   Folio Post at One Shilling each Quire.
>   Demy—— at Two Shillings
>   Medium at Three Shillings
>   Royal—— at Four Shillings
>   Super Royal at Six Shillings
>
> ## Paper for Printing
>
> News.   Almanacks.
>
> Double Crown at 14 s. each Ream.   Book—Crown Paper at 10 s. 6d.
> Double Demy at 19 s.   Book——Fools Cap at 6 s. 6d. each Ream.
>   Pocket — Folio Post at 20 s.
>   Sheet——Demy at 13 s.

The cost of paper and printing is listed on a 1765 pricing guide as a result of the British Stamp Act.

John Adams who, as a lawyer, used legal documents in his day-to-day work, was one of the many who were not too pleased. While he was happy about Great Britain's victory over the French, he was not at all happy about the British government's growing attempts to gain more control over the colonies. Whereas there was a time when he considered himself a loyal subject of the British Empire, he was now beginning to feel differently. If the British government continued its efforts, he realized, there would likely be some ugly clashes in the years ahead. And if it came to that, he would have to decide which side he would take.

Adams became highly respected for his views on the rights of colonists.

THE FIGHT FOR FREEDOM

$\mathcal{A}$dams decided to speak out against the Stamp Act and, in a larger sense, about the overall rights of the American colonists. He wrote an essay about how the colonists should have the same rights as the British citizens who lived in England. He feared that the British government was thinking of the colonists in North America as lesser citizens. His essay was published in a newspaper called the *Boston Gazette*, in August of 1765 and, as a result, Adams became famous throughout the Boston area. He wrote exactly what was on many people's minds, and he did it in such a clear and powerful way that many thought of him as brilliant. In one part of the essay he made his feelings clear on the subject of kings and rulers in general:

> In the earliest ages of the world, absolute monarchy seems to have been the universal form of government. Kings, and a few of their great counselors and captains, exercised a cruel tyranny over the people, who held a rank in the scale of intelligence, in those days, but little higher than the camels and elephants that carried them and their engines to war.

He also offered his opinion as to why his fellow colonists were languishing under Britain's rule:

The true source of our sufferings has been our timidity. We have been afraid to think. We have felt a reluctance to examining into the grounds of our privileges, and the extent in which we have an indisputable right to demand them, against all the power and authority on earth.

Then, amazingly, he did it again. In a second essay published in the *Gazette*, Adams said the Stamp Act and other new taxes instituted by the British government were unfair because the colonists weren't given the chance to agree to them. Adams wasn't saying the colonists should never be taxed, he was saying that they hadn't been allowed to participate in the *decision* to be taxed. To describe this, Adams used a phrase that has since become unforgettable in American history—"taxation without representation." People began thinking of Adams as a heroic man and a magnificent thinker. His ideas were bringing the colonists together and making them want to fight against the British government and its unfair practices.

And so in 1766, under tremendous pressure from the colonists, Parliament's leaders gave in and repealed the Stamp Act. But this didn't mean they were done trying to collect money through taxation. Angered by the way the

Boston, May. 17, 1766.

AT a Meeting of the Sons of Liberty, held last Evening in Hanover square, it was unanimously Voted,

1. That their Exhibition of Joy on the Repeal of the Stamp Act be on the Common.

2. That the Fire Works be play'd off from a Stage to be erected near the Work-House Gates.

3. That there be an Advertisement published on Monday next, of the intended Exhibition, the Place where, and the Time when it will end.

I do therefore notify the Friends

of Liberty, that an authentic Account of the Repeal of the Stamp Act is arrived, and the Gentlemen Select Men of *Boston*, have fix'd upon This Evening for the public Rejoicing, at whose Desire, will be exhibited on the Common, an *OBELISK* —A Description of which is engraved by Mr. *Paul Revere*; and is now selling by Edes and Gill.——The Signal of its Ending will be firing a Horizontal Wheel on the Top of the *Obelisk*, when its desired the Assembly would retire. *By Order of the Committe*, May 19, 1766. *(Signed) M. Y. Secretary.*

In May 1766 the Boston Gazette *ran the repeal of the Stamp Act.*

colonists fought the Stamp Act, they created the Townshend Acts the following year. This instituted a group of new rules that were even more unfair than those of the Stamp Act. For example, it required that the colonists pay taxes on many important day-to-day items brought to America from Britain, such as glass, paper goods, and tea.

The colonists were enraged, and once again they turned to Adams for help. Adams's law practice was doing very well by this time, and he was a busy man. He moved his family out of Braintree and up to Boston in 1768 because that was where he was spending most of his time. Again he wrote to express his strong feelings about the unfair practices of the British government, and again the colonists loved every word. The British leadership realized that Adams was becoming more and more popular—and that meant that Adams had power. So they offered him a job in the British-controlled courts in the hope that

STRANGERS IN THE HOUSE

The Townshend Acts also required colonists to open their homes to British soldiers who needed a place to live and to sleep. Many of these soldiers had been in the colonies since the French and Indian War, and they were supposed to be protecting the colonists from further attacks by Native Americans. But many colonists were fearful that these same soldiers would also force them to obey the Townshend Acts.

they could control him. Even though the job paid well and was considered very important, Adams saw what the British were trying to do, and he turned it down. In spite of all this he still hoped that the difficulties the colonists were having with the British government could be solved in a sensible and peaceful way. That hope began to fade on a cool March night in 1770.

THE FIRST DROPS OF BLOOD

Even though Adams understood how angry his fellow colonists felt toward the British leaders, he hated the idea of letting this anger drive anyone to violence. He believed that violent actions were to be a last resort—something you did only in defense, when someone was attacking you first. And most of the colonists agreed with him. Still, there were times when people's emotions became so strong that they had trouble controlling themselves. An example of this was a horrible and unfortunate incident called the Boston Massacre.

The British government, knowing that the colonists hated the Townshend Acts, deployed soldiers into the Boston area to force the colonists to obey them. But the colonists continued to ignore the Acts, and they often gave the British soldiers a hard time. This, of course, only made both sides angrier. Finally, tensions exploded on March 5, 1770, when a group of colonists gathered in a Boston square to protest the Acts. British soldiers hurried to the site to keep them under control. The colonists began throwing things at the soldiers. Fearing for their own safety, the soldiers took out their rifles and began firing. When the battle was over, five colonists lay dead.

The colonists demanded justice, and the soldiers were placed under arrest. Adams agreed to be the soldiers' lawyer

Angered by the British-imposed Townshend Acts, the residents of Boston took to the streets and battled British soldiers in what is now known as the Boston Massacre,

because he believed the colonists were wrong—they started the incident through their violent actions. In the end, all but two of the soldiers tried for murder were **acquitted**. And the two who were judged guilty were given only light punishments. Incredibly, Adams lost very little of his popularity among the colonists. They had come to trust him so much that most believed he had done the right thing. Nevertheless, a great deal of damage had been done to the relationship between the colonists and the British leaders. With five deaths at the hands of the British army, it would never be the same.

After the Boston Massacre trial, Adams's busy life became even busier. He was elected to a branch of government known as a legislature. The legislature was given the power to write new laws and to change laws that already existed. He didn't stay in that position long, however, because he was feeling overworked and exhausted. He and Abigail also had two more children— Charles, born in 1770, and Thomas, born in 1772. He moved his family back to Braintree, hoping to focus on only his wife, his children, and his law practice. He needed a break and promised himself he would not get involved in politics again.

THE BOSTON TEA PARTY

Adams managed to keep this promise for a while. But then came another important event in the history of America—the Boston Tea Party. By late 1773 the British government had given up on the idea of collecting most of the taxes they demanded by the Townshend Acts. But they did keep the tax on tea—mostly to let the colonists know the British government was still in charge. By this time, however, the enraged colonists were resolved to be free of British rule. In November three British ships sailed into Boston Harbor, loaded with over three hundred wooden chests of tea. The colonists refused to pay the tax on the tea and ordered that the ships go back to Britain. When the colonists were told that they had to pay the tax, they decided to take action. On the night of December 16 dozens of men dressed as Mohawk Indians (led by Samuel Adams, John's second cousin) boarded the ships, broke open the chests, and dumped the tea— thousands of pounds of it—into the harbor. Since no one was hurt during the incident, John Adams happily approved of it.

American colonists cheer as others, dressed as Native Americans, dump British tea into Boston Harbor during the Boston Tea Party.

The British government was, to no one's surprise, enraged. In response, it created yet another new set of rules and laws, this time aimed directly at the people of Massachusetts. They closed Boston Harbor so that no ships could deliver goods and supplies there. They also ordered the people to stop having town meetings—because those meetings usually ended up with the people more determined than ever to fight for their independence from Britain. These new rules were eventually called the Intolerable Acts, and they were created to make an example of the Massachusetts colonists. The British government hoped the Intolerable Acts would scare the people in other parts of the colony away from trying to break free from Britain.

But the colonists kept fighting back. On September 5, 1774, each colony sent a few delegates to Philadelphia to attend a meeting to discuss the problems the colonies were having with Great Britain. The group that met was called the First Continental Congress. Massachusetts chose Thomas Cushing, Robert Treat Paine, Samuel Adams, and John Adams to be delegates. Even at this stage most of the delegates were in favor of trying to find a way to mend their relationship with the British government. But first, they decided, they had to force Britain to repeal, or end, the Intolerable Acts. They decided to do this by refusing to do any more business with the British—stop selling goods that the colonists produced (clothing and tobacco, for example) while, at the same time not buying goods that the British produced and shipped to the colonies. Adams had several other ideas that were not agreed upon, including the creation of a formal colonial government that was not controlled by Great Britain. Unfortunately, he did not get enough delegates to agree to this idea, and it was rejected—at least for a time.

The meeting of the First Continental Congress ended on October 26, 1774, with the delegates hoping that their refusal to do business with Britain would put an end to the Intolerable Acts and the bad relationship between the colonies and the British government. But it didn't—a few months later, in two Massachusetts towns called Lexington and Concord, everything changed.

Patrick Henry, a delegate from Virginia, speaks out at the First Continental Congress, in 1774.

The American Revolution Begins

On April 14, 1775, the royal governor of Massachusetts, Thomas Gage, was ordered to find and seize a huge quantity of military supplies that the colonists had hidden in the town of Concord. Furthermore, Gage was to find and arrest the colonial leaders in the area—including Samuel Adams. Gage, who was also a general, gathered groups of soldiers and set out early in the evening of April 18. However, the plan did not work because several colonists had found out about it through spies they had placed on the British side. The military supplies were carefully hidden,

A militia of four hundred fought back almost twice as many British troops at the Battle of Concord.

and Samuel Adams escaped long before any British soldiers could get near him. Then the colonists formed their own armies, called militias, and gunfights broke out. The first battle was in Lexington, the second in Concord, as the colonial militias forced the British soldiers back and continued on through other nearby towns. By the next morning more than one hundred people were dead, and the American Revolution had begun. Everyone in the colonies then had to take a side—you were either with the colonists or you were with the British.

John Adams went to Philadelphia at the end of April to take part in the Second Continental Congress. This time there was a greater sense of urgency. The colonist's relationship with Great Britain was becoming bloodier and uglier. There were still some members of Congress who wanted to fix it, but not as many as before. One of the first matters this second Congress addressed was the need for the colonies to have their own official army. Adams recommended that George Washington be the leader of this army, and the other delegates agreed. Adams also said that the time had come for each colony to form its own government rather than continue to be ruled by British governors. This idea was also agreed upon.

The British leaders realized that the colonists were trying to break completely free of them. In response, they sent more soldiers, and the fighting continued. Amazingly, the colonial armies did very well in the early stages of the war. They attacked British troops in Boston and eventually forced them to flee into Canada. In the southern colonies American soldiers won battle after battle, capturing hundreds of British men and supplies. They failed to achieve similar success in Canada, mainly because they simply did not have enough soldiers or supplies to fight outside their own towns and cities. But they still achieved enough victories to gain support from the public and, perhaps more importantly, from the men in the Second Continental Congress who were making the crucial decisions about the nation's future.

THE PIECE OF PAPER THAT CHANGED EVERYTHING

In June of 1776 most delegates in Congress decided that the time had come for the people of America to tell the British government that they no longer recognized its authority—that America was its own country run by its own people and no one else. Adams, Benjamin Franklin, and a delegate from Virginia named Thomas Jefferson were asked to draft the document that would become known as the Declaration of Independence. After some discussion Adams and Franklin decided to have Jefferson come up with the actual wording, as his writing skills were known to be superb.

After Jefferson finished the first draft, however, there was plenty of arguing among the other delegates about what should be removed, what should be added, how certain things should be worded, and so on. The strongest arguments came from the few delegates who still hoped the colonies could somehow repair their relationship with Great Britain. It was John Adams, not Thomas Jefferson, who eventually convinced even these people that the declaration needed to be issued. It was adopted by all delegates on July 4, 1776.

The Revolutionary War became more difficult for colonial forces after the Declaration of Independence was signed. Thousands of new British soldiers, arriving from Europe by boat, attacked George Washington's army in New York. These soldiers were well trained and better equipped than the colonial forces, and Washington's army was forced to retreat. Adams, along with

Benjamin Franklin, John Adams (center), and Thomas Jefferson worked closely on the Declaration of Independence.

four other members of Congress, formed a committee known as the Board of War. It was essentially their job to manage and oversee every aspect of the war effort. They issued soliders' pay, decided on promotions, and ensured that there were enough guns, bullets, uniforms, tents, and wagons. Adams was given the task of heading this committee, in spite of his many other responsibilities consuming much of his time through 1777. Meanwhile, the British were gaining ground in parts of New Jersey, Rhode Island, and Canada. Then, in September and October of 1777, they invaded Pennsylvania. The Continental Congress had, by this time, left Philadelphia to find safety.

General George Washington's army wintered at Valley Forge, Pennsylvania in 1777, under horrible conditions.

The lowest point in the war for Washington and his army was the winter of 1777. He led his weary soldiers to Valley Forge, an area roughly 20 miles from Philadelphia, to spend the winter. Very little fighting could be done during these months, so he hoped they would have a chance to rest and prepare for more battles in the spring. Instead, with all the snow and ice, and with the Continental Congress unable to send supplies, Washington's men suffered horribly. They did not have enough warm clothes, food, or medicine. Numerous diseases, such as typhoid, pneumonia, and dysentery, left many of them dead, as did starvation and exposure. Also, with no money, the surviving soldiers couldn't even be paid. Some deserted, which meant they simply left, with no intention of fighting anymore. Those who stayed became disinterested and saddened. General Washington feared that by the spring, he would have no army left to fight with.

Then, in February of 1778, Baron Friedrich Wilhelm von Steuben arrived at Valley Forge. He was a brilliant Prussian military officer working for France, and he offered to teach Washington's troops better ways of fighting. By the time the winter freeze began to thaw, the colonial army was better trained. Then, finally, supplies started arriving. At last things were getting better.

A TURNING POINT IN THE WAR

British military leaders decided they had to capture the colonial city of Albany, in New York. By doing this, they would weaken the colonial army, and they would also have control of one of the colonists' most important business centers. In order to achieve this, they sent several army divisions toward Albany from different directions. One of the largest and strongest was led by a British general named John Burgoyne. As he moved his men closer to Albany in July of 1777, he expected other British divisions to meet him there, thus surrounding the city and crushing the colonial forces.

However, the other British divisions were successfully fought back by divisions of the colonial army, making General Burgoyne's job much more difficult. By September, Burgoyne's men had made their way through the town of Saratoga, not far from Albany, but this was where their progress stopped. Colonial soldiers, now better able to fight, thanks to the excellent training from von Steuben, forced Burgoyne back to Saratoga. Now Burgoyne's division had less than six thousand men, whereas the colonial army had nearly three times as many. In mid-October Burgoyne had no choice but to surrender.

JOHN ADAMS IN FRANCE

The American victory at Saratoga not only lifted the spirits of Washington's men, it also proved that the colonists had some chance of winning the war. Throughout much of the fighting, the French government had been secretly sending military supplies to the colonists. They were still angry over Britain's victory in the French and Indian War, during which they lost so much of their land in North America.

Adams, along with Benjamin Franklin and others, went to France to ask for more money, plus full recognition of the American colonies as a free and independent nation. Adams made the ocean journey with his eleven-year-old son, John Quincy. It was on this ship that the two Adamses began learning French, as most of the other travelers were French soldiers returning home. Once in France, John made sure that John Quincy was enrolled in school so he could continue his education. Father and son also attended plays and social events together, and they lived with Benjamin Franklin.

The French, impressed by the news of recent colonial victories—particularly the one at Saratoga—agreed to these requests and even offered to participate in the actual fighting of the war. They promised more money, more supplies, and the use of not only their army but also their navy to help battle the British at sea.

John Adams, Benjamin Franklin, and others appeared before King Louis XVI of France, seeking financial support for the colonies in their battle with England.

The British, realizing that they were now facing much stronger forces and could possibly lose the war altogether, tried to offer the colonists a deal—they would repeal all the taxes and unfair laws they had tried to force on the colonies before, and in return the colonies would go back to being part of the British Empire. But it was too late for any of this—Adams and the rest of the colonial leaders rejected the idea. They wanted full independence.

The Beginning of the End

The loss at Saratoga had dealt the British a devastating blow, but the war was far from over. The British decided to change their plans for defeating the colonists. During the summer of 1778 they moved their troops out of Philadelphia and into New York and Rhode Island. Then, in the autumn, they also went after some of the southern colonies. They felt there were more people in the South who still wanted to make peace with the British government. And they were right—using a combination of their own soldiers and colonists who were still loyal to them, called Loyalists, they soon captured major cities in Georgia and South Carolina. These areas were also valuable because of their rich farmland.

The problem the British had with their plans to conquer the South was not that they couldn't capture those areas in the first place—it was that they couldn't hold on to them afterward. Their army had been weakened by being broken into too many pieces, with some in the northern colonies, some in the southern colonies, and some trying to protect British interests in other parts of the country. The colonists, with help from the French, continued fighting back. Even though they didn't win every battle, they gradually wore the British down. They also succeeded in cutting off the flow of important supplies to the British troops. The powerful French navy, along with the smaller colonial navy (which included ordinary people fighting from small, private boats), constantly attacked British ships. Tons of supplies sank to the bottom of the ocean—supplies the British soldiers desperately needed.

While all this was going on, John Adams kept himself busy. He left Europe in the summer of 1779 and returned to Massachusetts, where he was asked to write the state's new constitution. With his congressional experience, his extensive legal training, and his idealistic and moralistic views on society and the human race, he was perfect for the job. The document he eventually created became revered among the population of Massachusetts. It largely reflected the best ideas of similar works, ensuring the rights of the citizens while outlining the structure and philosophy of an effective, subservient government. It is to Adams's credit that this work still stands, largely unchanged, today. It is the oldest state constitution in the United States.

In October of 1779 Adams was sent back to Europe by Congress, this time to the Netherlands. And he brought along some company again—his sons John Quincy and the younger Charles. Interestingly, the journey was a treacherous one that might have changed the course of American history—the ship upon which they were traveling, called the *Sensible*, began leaking when it was in the middle of the Atlantic Ocean. Then a storm hit. For weeks the passengers and crew feared for their lives, pumping and bucketing water overboard as the leak grew worse. Then, miraculously, the shores of Spain appeared on the horizon, and the *Sensible* sailed toward it. From there Adams

Adams spent a great deal of time overseas, forging relationships with other countries.

and his two boys were forced to take a rocky and difficult land route to their destination. It was an experience none of them would soon forget.

Adams's goal in the Netherlands was the same as it had been in France—to ask the Dutch for loans and to recognize America as an independent nation. The Dutch had had their own troubles with the British—their own ships carrying goods had been attacked by Britain's navy in years past. So they were willing to consider Adams's request for help. But they were also hesitant—what if the colonists lost the war? If that happened, they would be loaning money that they would never get back, and they would be investing it in a nation that didn't even exist. Their worries were cast aside when Adams, while still in the Netherlands, received amazing news.

THE FINAL BATTLES

The British, realizing they had no hope of holding onto the southern colonies, moved their forces north, stopping in Yorktown, Virginia. They hoped to rest, regroup, and build a base from which they could launch new attacks. But George Washington had no intention of letting that happen. With the help of the French, he and his men continued to attack British divisions in the North and cut off their supplies. The soldiers in Yorktown were the only hope Great Britain had left—but Washington's army, along with thousands of French soldiers, surrounded them. In September of 1781 the commander of the British forces, Charles Cornwallis, realized he was hopelessly outnumbered—his tired and poorly supplied force of more than 7,000 men were up against about 18,000 led by General Washington. Knowing all

The Treaty of Paris, *painted by Benjamin West, remains unfinished because the British Peace Commission refused to pose for the painting.*

was lost, he surrendered. Adams happily reported this news to the Dutch, who were then willing to grant the colonists loans and to recognize America as its own country.

Unfortunately for Adams, the end of the fighting on the battlefields didn't automatically mean the end of struggles elsewhere.

He, along with others who had been sent to Europe by Congress, still had to get Great Britain, France, and Spain to sign treaties. All three nations were willing to do so—but only under certain conditions. What made this even more complicated was that each nation wanted something different in return. The French, for example, wanted to take back many of the islands in the West Indies that were rich in sugar and other agricultural goods, which they'd lost during the French and Indian War. Spain wanted Britain to give up its claim to Gibraltar, a small area of land that controlled passage into the Mediterranean Sea. But Britain, of course, did not want to give up any of these things. Adams pushed hard during the negotiations, interested only in what was best for his new country. Eventually, all sides found terms they could live with, and they collectively signed the Treaty of Paris on September 3, 1783.

The Revolutionary War was over.

Adams was presented to King George III as the American ambassador to the English court.

A YOUNG NATION

Four

$\mathcal{A}$dams remained in Europe after signing the Treaty of Paris. In June of 1784 his wife, Abigail, and daughter, Nabby, sailed from America to be with him. They rented a house in Paris and, as a family, generally enjoyed French life. Adams also continued working to improve America, asking for more money and making other agreements with the governments of France and Holland. The Adamses also spent time with Thomas Jefferson. Like Adams, Jefferson was living in France and representing the new American nation.

In April of 1785 Adams received a letter from Congress asking him to move to London—he now had to represent America in England. He and his family left Paris in May, a sad day for them and for the many friends they left behind. Not long after they arrived in London, Adams met with the British king, George III. Although the two men had many things in common and could have built a friendship under different circumstances, they were on opposite sides of a still-difficult relationship. King George was the leader of the country that Adams's country had just beaten in a bloody war. This first meeting was brief and polite, but there was still anger under the surface. In fact, both Adams and his wife would say that they received similar receptions from the everyday people they met—the English were polite on the outside, but nothing more than that. Adams also noticed many of the English seemed to believe that, sooner or later, the United States of America would want to be ruled by Britain again. Adams found this ridiculous.

What irritated Adams even more, however, was his lack of progress in dealing with the British leadership. He had been sent to England mostly to resolve problems created by the Treaty of Paris. Some of the issues involved the money that the United States owed the British, the removal of the last of British soldiers still in America, and payment for American property that was destroyed or seized during the Revolutionary War. Also, the United States wanted to agree on terms under which it could trade with Great Britain. The main reason for this lack of progress, Adams soon realized, was that British leaders knew America was still a weak country, unable to fight for itself. So they felt they didn't have to honor the Treaty of Paris.

THE CONSTITUTION

Back in America, the end of the war was causing other problems throughout the thirteen states. Perhaps the greatest was the cost. Wars are expensive affairs, and Congress, as well as the governments of each state, owed millions of dollars. Some was from foreign countries that helped the colonists during the war. Money was also owed to the colonists themselves, who either served in the war without pay, gave money of their own to help the military buy equipment, or freely gave goods and services with the agreement that they would be paid later on. Farmers were struggling particularly hard, as they needed money from the government to keep their farms going. They, too, had helped with the war effort, often supplying food that they could otherwise have sold for a profit.

At that time each of America's thirteen colonies still governed itself. That meant there wasn't one strong central

THE ARTICLES OF CONFEDERATION

The thirteen states were already working together in honor of a kind of friendship agreement between them called the Articles of Confederation. It was adopted in 1777 and acted as a kind of guide for

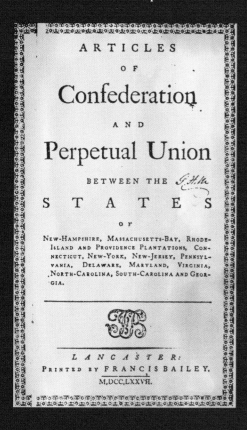

governing. It outlined rules on how the states could go about waging war or building relationships with foreign countries, printing money for domestic use, and dealing with important political issues. It was created to keep the states together during the Revolutionary War, so they would act as one nation in battle against Great Britain. But once the war ended, the Articles of Confederation were no longer useful—America needed a government with control over all states, and in turn it needed some kind of agreement with the states to allow this.

government, but rather thirteen separate governments. So on May 25, 1787, fifty-five state delegates met in Philadelphia for the Constitutional Convention. The group included some of the most important and respected men of the time, including George Washington, Alexander Hamilton, and Benjamin Franklin. John Adams, along with his friend Thomas Jefferson, was still in Europe and could not attend. But their influence was strong among the other delegates, so many of their ideas and beliefs were represented in their absence.

BUILDING A GOVERNMENT

The delegates worked quickly to design their proposed central government. One of the most important decisions they made was to divide governmental power into separate pieces, making it impossible for one person or group to have too much. There would be three parts, or branches, of the new federal government. The executive branch would be led by a person called the president. The legislative branch would create all new laws. It would be run by the U.S. Congress, which would be split into two houses—a Senate and a House of Representatives. And finally there would be a judicial branch, responsible for interpreting the laws created by Congress. This branch would be headed by the Supreme Court—a group of judges of great wisdom and experience, appointed by the president and approved by Congress.

There were many other details to the document in which these ideas were written, called the Constitution, and nine out of the thirteen states had to agree upon them in order for the Constitution to be passed. Nevertheless, the delegates wanted *all* thirteen states to approve it. This would not be done, however, until some amendments, or changes, to the Constitution were made. The first ten amendments eventually became known as the Bill of Rights. Their purpose was, specifically, to make sure the federal government never became too powerful. The American people didn't want another autocratic government like the one they just broke away from in Britain. The Constitution itself was finally ratified by the last of the thirteen states—Rhode Island—in 1790, putting the new federal government in place. The Bill of Rights was fully ratified a year later.

Adams Returns Home

Adams did his best to convince the British to honor the terms of the Treaty of Paris. Eventually, he realized he was making no progress, so he decided to go back to America. He set sail in April of 1788 and landed in Boston on June 17. His plans at the time were simple—get back to Braintree, spend time with his family, and grow to be a happy old man. He had been out of his beloved country for almost ten years, and it was time to relax. Destiny, however, would lead him in a very different direction.

The moment Adams's ship came into view, cannons were fired to let the citizens know of his arrival. Whereas the states-man often felt mistreated by the people of Great Britain, he found a very different crowd waiting for him in Boston. Thousands of cheering people packed the shore, and bells rang out to honor the man they considered a hero. The governor of Massachusetts sent a carriage to take Adams and his wife to his mansion for a celebration dinner. Soon Adams was meeting with old friends again, feeling happier than he had in ages. He also had the chance to see his two younger sons, Charles and Thomas, who, like their father, had gone to Harvard.

This portrait of John Adams was painted in approximately 1788, when he returned to America from Great Britain.

Back in Braintree, Adams moved into a large and beautiful mansion that he'd purchased the previous year while still in Great Britain. He would eventually name his home Peacefield and spend a great deal of time and money expanding it. It seemed he was, at last, at age 53, settling down. But then there was talk of his future in government affairs. He had played such an important role in the birth of America, helping the people gain freedom from Great Britain. Surely he would not retire from politics now—surely he would play *some* role in the new government.

AMERICA'S FIRST VICE PRESIDENT

With the ratification of the Constitution came the need for the United States to elect its first president. Therefore, there was also the need for a vice president. The leaders of the nation had already accepted the fact that George Washington was the perfect choice for the presidency. He was so popular and so highly regarded, it was hard to think of anyone else in the position. But who would fill the role of vice president?

There were no political parties at the time—one party did not choose a candidate to run in an election against a candidate from another party, as is done today. Instead, the president was chosen through a system set up by the Constitution called the electoral college. The electoral college was a group of delegates from each state, and they had to cast votes for the two people they felt would make the best president. The person who received the most votes became president, and the person who came in second became the vice president. George Washington received the most votes from the electoral college of 1789, and John Adams was the runner-up.

The vice president's duties didn't seem very exciting to Adams. First and foremost he had to be ready to take over the presidency in the event that the sitting president died. Also, he was the leader of the Senate, where many new laws and policies would be created. While this could have been very interesting to Adams, the vice president's role as defined by the Constitution did not allow him to actually take part in any law-making debates or discussions—he was only supposed to *oversee* them as they were carried out by the other members of the Senate. The only time he would have some say was when exactly half the Senate voted one way, and the other half voted the other way. It would then be the vice president's job to cast the deciding vote.

SETTING THINGS UP

President Washington quickly realized he had a lot of setting-up to do with his new government and new nation. He was sworn in as president on April 30, 1789, and went right to work. He organized several departments to deal with different matters of importance. There was a Department of State (originally called the Department of Foreign Affairs), a Department of War, and a Department of the Treasury.

Washington wanted to appoint wise and experienced people to run these departments. For the Department of State, which would handle America's relationship with other countries, he chose Thomas Jefferson. For the Department of War, which managed military matters, he chose Henry Knox, who had served with Washington during the Revolutionary War. And for the Department of the Treasury, which handled the country's

*George Washington
was inaugurated
in New York City
in 1789.
John Adams
was his vice
president.*

financial matters, he chose Alexander Hamilton. Hamilton also had served with Washington in the war, and he had a brilliant mind for economics.

Hamilton would play a particularly important role in Washington's first term as president. He put together a plan to deal with the massive debt the nation had acquired through waging the Revolutionary War. Congress debated long and hard over Hamilton's plan, but it was eventually approved—the federal government would pay the money owed by the individual states, and it would also ask for new loans from foreign countries. Hamilton also wanted to create a new bank, one that belonged to the government. There was some question over whether this could be done according to the rules of the Constitution. But Washington thought it was a good idea—he didn't think the new government could function without its own bank.

LITTLE TO DO

Adams gave advice to President Washington from time to time, although only when Washington asked for it. Adams felt it was part of the vice president's job to faithfully support the president's ideas and policies. If, for example, Adams had to cast a tiebreaking vote in the Senate, he would vote in whatever way helped Washington. It is important to note that Adams did not seem to have any strong opinions about the people that Washington had chosen to head his departments. At that point in his life, Adams got along well with all of these men—but that would change in the years ahead.

With little to do, Adams quickly became bored with the vice presidency. He once called it "the most insignificant office that ever the invention of man contrived." He did, however, become deeply involved in one matter—that of how the president should be addressed. Adams, who had lived in Europe for so long in countries that had royal leaders, believed strongly in high-sounding titles, such as His Excellency and His Highness. But most others felt that, having just broken free of Great Britain, more humble titles were better. James Madison, a member of the House of Representatives (and eventually the fourth president), said, "The more simple, the more republican we are in our manners, the more national dignity we shall acquire." Adams was mocked for his love of grand titles. His peers ignored his suggestions and settled on the basic title President of the United States.

REFLECTION

By 1792 Washington, who had given so much of his time, talents, and energy to the shaping of the new nation, was ready to retire to his beautiful home, Mount Vernon. However, many people had grave concerns about whether this would be good for the health of the country. The states in the North were having frequent disagreements with the states in the South concerning important matters. Also, people inside the government were taking different sides on many issues, which meant separate political parties might soon form. With the country so young, Washington feared that if he left his office, everything might fall apart. In spite of all the disagreements and arguments, everyone still liked Washington and believed in his leadership. So in spite of his weariness, he agreed to be president for another four years. And John Adams was again chosen to be the vice president.

This political cartoon from 1792 satirizes King Louis the XVI of France as a worthless pig.

The first major issue Washington faced in his second term was the **French Revolution**. For years the people of France had been growing more and more dissatisfied with their royal leadership. They were making less money, while the cost of living grew ever higher. There were riots in the street, and fighting in and around government offices and royal palaces. Finally, the angry French citizens reached a point where they could take no more, and they removed their king—Louis XVI—from power (even going so far as to cut off his head). Now France was ruled not by a king but by the people, and the new French government quickly declared war on four other European nations—Austria, England, Prussia, and Spain.

Adams was alarmed by the French Revolution. Just as he had done before the American Revolution, he wrote a series of newspaper essays about it. But, unlike his attitude toward the American fight, his opinion of the French uprising was more critical and negative. He felt the French rebels would grow out of control and that whatever new government they formed would be unable to lead the country. A lot of people were disappointed by this, wondering if Adams had forgotten what it was like to be at the mercy of a cruel government.

The new leaders of France asked America for help in their war against the other European countries. President Washington was in a difficult spot—a treaty had been signed with King Louis XVI in 1778 offering assistance to France in the event of any war. And France's help undoubtedly played a key role in America's victory over the British in the American Revolution. But in spite of all this, Washington decided to take no sides—he felt his young country was still too fragile to become involved in yet another messy conflict.

BREAKING INTO PIECES

Just when it seemed that America was starting to come together as a nation, its government began to come apart. Washington, when selecting men to run each of the executive departments, had wanted to be fair and choose people with different viewpoints.

The problem with that, however, was that these men eventually began to disagree with each other on many issues.

Washington became deeply concerned about these disagreements. Hamilton and Jefferson in particular seemed to be going against each other all the time. Washington felt that people in government were supposed to work together to serve the best interests of the American people. That meant sometimes setting aside one's personal feelings. But Hamilton and Jefferson had trouble doing this. Slowly, two separate political parties began to form.

Hamilton eventually led the Federalist Party, whose members believed that most political power should be held by a nation's government. Jefferson, on the other hand, helped build the Republican Party—soon after called the Democratic-Republican Party (not related to the present-day party). He believed that the people should have most of the ruling power, not the government. President Washington eventually accepted the fact that this division among his own people had taken place, but he was never happy about it. Adams, for the most part, was a Federalist, and this would eventually do great damage to his long friendship with Thomas Jefferson.

Adams continued supporting Washington's policies during their second term. Washington built solid relationships with many foreign nations in an attempt to strengthen America's position around the world. He signed treaties with Spain and Algiers, plus a new one with Great Britain—which enraged many Americans who remembered how the British had refused to honor the terms of the Treaty of Paris. But Washington was pleased because the new treaty made certain that America would not be

This 1793 cartoon ridicules the anti-Federalists as an unruly mob opposed to government.

pulled into another war. It also set the relationship with Great Britain on the right track at last. There was also a treaty with Native Americans living in the northwestern part of the country. It gave Americans permission to begin moving west, out of the thirteen states and into new territory.

WASHINGTON SAYS GOOD-BYE

By mid-1796 George Washington had had enough. He made it clear to all that he would not, under any circumstances, allow himself to be elected to a third term. He felt America was stable enough to be handed over to someone else and, in September, he finished his Farewell Address, which was then published in a Philadelphia newspaper called the *American Daily Advertiser*. It is still considered one of the most powerful presidential statements in American history. With Washington's personal future clear, the nation needed a new man to take his place at the helm of government.

The Second President of the United States *Five*

$\mathcal{W}$hereas the first two American presidential elections were fairly quiet, dignified affairs, the election of 1796 was the exact opposite. George Washington was a national hero, beloved by one and all. But different political parties had formed, and people were taking sides. John Adams, being the vice president, seemed the obvious next choice for the position. But others were also mentioned—Thomas Jefferson, for example, was leading the Republican Party and had many supporters. Since Adams was considered a Federalist, Jefferson, his old and dear friend, was a political rival. There were two others who had their chances, too—Thomas Pinckney and Aaron Burr. But neither had the support of the people, so it really came down to Adams or Jefferson.

Hamilton, many historians believe, wanted the presidency for himself. But since he was also unpopular with the public, he realized he would not win enough votes through the electoral college. Instead, he decided to support Pinckney. He felt Pinckney was the kind of man he could control through charm and persuasion, so Pinckney would make a perfect president. When it seemed as though Adams would end up winning, however, Hamilton tried to get the electors to choose Pinckney as vice president instead. His motto seemed to be "Anyone but Jefferson," his bitter enemy. But in the end his plan failed—John

Although Alexander Hamilton tried to keep Thomas Jefferson (right) from the vice presidency, his efforts failed when Jefferson took a close second to John Adams in electoral votes, thus becoming the vice president.

Adams, with seventy-one electoral votes, became the new president, and Thomas Jefferson, close behind with sixty-eight votes, became the vice president. Interestingly, it was the only time in American history that the president and vice president were members of different political parties.

Even though Adams and Jefferson were in different parties, they did their best at the beginning of their political partnership to renew their friendship. They visited with each other shortly after the election to discuss the most important issues they would have to face together. Both men hoped that they could perform their jobs above and beyond the distractions of political rivalry. Surely the people who followed Jefferson in the past would want him to push for things that were different from those Adams and his followers wanted. But the two men agreed it would be in the best interest of the country to work in harmony and find agreeable solutions. The nation was doing well at this point—there was peace, there was work, and there was money. Most people lived comfortably and seemed content. Adams and Jefferson hoped to keep it that way. Unfortunately, their attempt at political friendship didn't last long. They had very different feelings about what role America should play in the ongoing battle between France and Great Britain.

TRYING TO STAY OUT OF IT

President Adams hoped to avoid having America dragged into the French-British conflict. The former president, George Washington, had decided, even against the outcry of the American people, that the country had been through enough fighting in recent years, and he didn't want to get involved. Adams supported Washington's policy as vice president, and now he wanted to continue it. But many disagreed with him, and for several different reasons. Jefferson and his Republicans, for example, thought the people of France had every right to fight Great Britain. Jefferson admired their willingness to stand up for themselves. But many Federalists—those who were being influenced by Alexander Hamilton, even though he wasn't even in a governmental position anymore—thought it better for America to take Great Britain's side.

Both the British and the French were upset by America's unwillingness to take part in the war. They began attacking or seizing American ships, which were simply trying to trade goods with each country. American sailors were being killed, and thousands of dollars' worth of merchandise was being stolen. Soon the American people were demanding action as well. Adams, feeling pressure from every direction, called Congress together to work out a solution. He still wanted peace, he told them, and suggested sending three diplomats to France to work out a new treaty. The members of Congress agreed that this was a sensible idea, and the three men set sail in early summer of 1797.

The XYZ Affair

President Adams was hopeful that the three diplomats could forge a renewed relationship with France and avoid the war. But not long after the group arrived, they encountered some problems. First, the leaders of the new French government refused to even see them. Then, they were permitted to meet, for only fifteen minutes, the French foreign minister Charles-Maurice de

French statesman Charles-Maurice de Talleyrand-Périgord attempted to bribe American diplomats in the X Y Z Affair.

Talleyrand-Périgord. The American diplomats told him why they had come, and he listened politely but gave no indication of whether he wanted a friendship with America or not. The diplomats left feeling confused and uncertain.

Then some days later, they were visited by three other men—French agents acting on behalf of Talleyrand. They said that Talleyrand would be willing to work out a new treaty with America, but only under two conditions—first, that Talleyrand personally be given $250,000, and second, that the nation of France be loaned $12 million. The American diplomats were outraged that the minister wanted a bribe and that the nation of France wanted to "buy" American friendship. They sent letters back to President Adams telling him of the situation, referring to the three agents as "X," "Y," and "Z" rather than using their actual names.

Adams's first reaction was to tell Congress only that the diplomatic mission had failed. But Thomas Jefferson wondered if Adams were holding back information—something that would make the French look good in the eyes of the American people. Maybe Adams was doing this because so many Federalists actually *wanted* war with France. Jefferson and other Republicans insisted that Adams tell the whole story. Adams waited as long as he could, then stepped before Congress and told the full truth. Jefferson realized he'd made a serious mistake—when the story of Talleyrand's attempted bribe and forced loan became public, anger toward France was greater than ever. Jefferson and his Republicans, who had been telling everyone to support France, suddenly looked foolish. Jefferson realized, too late, that Adams had withheld the information simply because he still wanted to avoid war with the French.

In preparation for possible conflict with France, Congress ordered that warships be built.

Along with Congress, Adams reluctantly ordered that an army be assembled and ready to go at a moment's notice. George Washington was asked to lead them if fighting was unavoidable. Washington agreed, and he wanted Alexander Hamilton to be his second in command. Adams hated the idea, but he didn't feel he had the right to oppose a former president and a beloved national hero. Finally, Adams and Congress created the Department of the Navy and ordered the immediate building of warships in order to engage in battle on the high seas.

The Final Step Toward Peace

Now that the feelings toward France were more hostile than ever, Alexander Hamilton pushed harder for America to go to war. He loved the idea that Thomas Jefferson and his Republican Party had been embarrassed by the French's attempted trickery. Hamilton still did not have an official governmental position, particularly since Washington's army had not yet been sent into battle. Still, Hamilton had great influence among many governmental officials, even among the secretaries of the war, treasury, and state departments.

The people who led these departments, as a group, were part of what was called the president's cabinet. Adams used the same men that Washington did—since America was still a young country, he didn't think it was a good idea to appoint new people to his own presidential cabinet. The problem was that a few of these cabinet members, now that Washington was gone, had decided to be more loyal to Hamilton than to Adams. If Adams made a decision that Hamilton didn't like, Hamilton would instruct these men to ignore Adams.

When President Adams realized the situation with France was getting out of hand, he did not discuss it with his cabinet. Some members were still on his side, but others weren't, and those men could not be trusted. So in a move that Hamilton did not see coming, Adams made one more attempt to ease the

Alexander Hamilton supported a war with France and tried to influence other members of the government.

growing tensions with France in a peaceful way. Still without first discussing it with anyone, Adams sent over a diplomat named William Vans Murray. He did this largely because one of the American diplomats who had been in France earlier, a man named John Marshall, had returned to tell Adams that, in his opinion, the French didn't really want war with America, either. Relieved, Adams sent Murray and hoped for the best.

Hamilton was outraged. He could no longer push for war with France now, because then the American people would see that he *wanted* war. What made the situation worse for him was that Murray, along with two other diplomats, did eventually work out a new treaty with France. The American people were thrilled, and Adams looked like a hero. Even Thomas Jefferson was pleased. But Alexander Hamilton, who controlled the half of the Federalist Party that didn't support John Adams, was bitter and angry. He would hate the president for the rest of his life.

THE ALIEN AND SEDITION ACTS

In spite of the many challenges faced by Adams during his presidency, most historians feel that, overall, he acted with decency, honor, and wisdom, with the best interests of his country at heart. One of the few times he did seem to make a mistake, however, was when he approved a set of laws that became known as the Alien and Sedition Acts.

An alien, by definition, was any person from another country who came to America. A visiting French citizen, for example, was considered an alien. And the word sedition described the practice of encouraging rebellion against a government.

THE FIRST PRESIDENT OF THE WHITE HOUSE

John Adams was the first president to live in the White House. However, he didn't move in until the last few months of his presidency. Previously, he and his wife had lived in a mansion on Market Street, in Philadelphia. There were no furnishings or decorations when Adams arrived at the White House and very little in the way of other buildings in the area. The nation's new capital at this point was little more than forest and swampland. But Adams found the president's new home to his liking and even wrote about it—"I pray Heaven to Bestow the best of blessings on this house, And All that shall hereafter inhabit it. May none but Honest and Wise men ever rule under This Roof." These words are now carved on the mantel of the State Dining Room.

In 1798 the Alien and Sedition Acts became law. They were a set of four laws, three of which dealt with potentially dangerous aliens in the United States, and the other addressing the problem of what the government, which was mostly Federalist, saw as a threat to its authority by the Jefferson-led Republicans, who criticized them through newspapers, pamphlets, and public speeches.

The three alien-related laws seemed to make sense to the American people, since there were many citizens from foreign countries trying to persuade Americans to get involved in the war in Europe. First, there was the Alien Enemies Act, which gave Adams the power to **deport** any aliens who came from a country that was at war against America. Then, there was the Alien Friends Act, which allowed the president to deport *anyone* from a foreign country who was deemed a threat. Finally, there was the Naturalization Act, which required an alien to live in America for fourteen years before being given American citizenship (before this, the required time was only five years).

It wasn't so much these three laws that upset the American public but the fourth—the Sedition Act. Through the threat of imprisonment and fines as high as $5,000 (a huge amount in 1798), people were forbidden to say or write anything that went against what the government said, believed, or was trying to do.

Thomas Jefferson and the rest of the Republicans were outraged by the Sedition Act. Since Adams's Federalist Party had most of the power in the government, Jefferson saw this as an attempt by Adams and the other Federalists to keep the Republicans from being heard by the public. The Republicans suspected the Federalists of trying to ensure that the American people heard from only one party—their own. Furthermore, the Republicans felt the Sedition Act violated one of the most basic promises made to the American people by the government in the First Amendment of the Bill of Rights—the right of free speech.

To be fair, President Adams rarely used the power he was given through the Alien and Sedition Acts. And, history suggests, he wasn't really interested in trying to stop ordinary people from speaking their minds. The only time these laws were used, it seems, was when newspaper editors or reporters printed what amounted to outright lies about what Adams's government was doing. Adams considered this a threat to the safety of the country, and he may only have been trying to protect his efforts and those of the people who supported him. Still, a great deal of damage was done to Adams's reputation and to the strength of his party. So many people were angered by the Alien and Sedition Acts that they decided to strike back at the Federalist Party in the next election.

The Election of 1800

Adams further weakened the Federalist Party by getting rid of two members of his cabinet—Timothy Pickering, Secretary of State, and James McHenry, Secretary of War. These two men, Adams long knew, were followers of Alexander Hamilton rather than himself, and he didn't want advisers that he couldn't trust. While he felt this was something he had to do, it made the American people feel even less confident in the strength of the Federalists.

A presidential campaign poster from the 1800 election supports Thomas Jefferson for president and proclaims, "John Adams No More."

When the time came for the election of 1800, Adams was once again the candidate of choice of the Federalists. He was already the president, which gave him a certain appeal, and he obviously had the experience and intelligence to handle the job. But Hamilton couldn't stand the thought of Adams serving as president for four more years, so he supported a man from South Carolina named Charles Cotesworth Pinckney. The Republicans, on the other hand, chose Thomas Jefferson and Aaron Burr as their two candidates. They also changed their name to the Democratic-Republicans.

In the end, Hamilton's plan once again turned against him—by taking away so much support for Adams and splitting the Federalist Party, Jefferson—another Hamilton enemy—ended up winning the election.

FINAL YEARS

John Adams was so deeply hurt by the election of 1800 that he didn't even attend Thomas Jefferson's swearing-in ceremony. Unlike the man who had held the presidency before him, George Washington, Adams had been attacked by various enemies almost from his first day in office. Washington didn't have to deal with the constant underhandedness of Alexander Hamilton, or from a cabinet he couldn't trust. And yet, in spite of all this, Adams always did what he believed to be best for his beloved country. He managed to create peace with a country, France, that, at times, seemed as though it wanted war with America, and even when a good portion of the American people wanted a war with it. He built a powerful navy from nothing, created a nation that was wealthy and productive, and carried himself with the kind of dignity that set the standard for all future presidents.

KEEPING BUSY

Adams arrived back in Massachusetts in March of 1801. Although he was sixty-five years old, he still felt young and full of life. He worried over what he would do with himself now that he had nothing to occupy his time. He and his wife, Abigail, were certain, however, that they wanted no further involvement in politics or government.

For a while Adams busied himself with farming again, while Abigail took care of the household matters such as cooking and washing. In many ways this was a return to the simple life they

Adams returned to his Braintree, Massachusetts, home after the loss of the 1800 election.

enjoyed in their younger years. And by all accounts Adams enjoyed it tremendously. He worked right alongside other farmhands during the day, doing his share of the labor and enjoying the exercise and fresh air. At night he would take up another of his old hobbies, reading, while collecting books by the thousands, eventually amassing a huge personal library.

LETTERS

John Adams always enjoyed hearing from his old friends. Back in those days the only way to communicate was by writing letters.

LETTERS TO ANOTHER OLD FRIEND

At the start of 1812 Adams took a moment to write a brief letter to someone else from his past—Thomas Jefferson. Jefferson was finished with the presidency by then and had retired to his home in Monticello, Virginia. The two men had not exchanged a single word in eleven years, and there were days when Adams was deeply bothered by this. They were the closest of friends as young men, fighting together for the cause of American independence against the British. But politics tore their friendship apart. Now Adams decided it was time to heal the old wounds. It did not take long for them to begin writing back and forth constantly, just as Adams did with Benjamin Rush, discussing many different subjects. They would all remain friends until the ends of their lives.

Adams did this several times a week, to many people—but his favorite, most likely, was Benjamin Rush. Rush, born in 1745, was one of the most accomplished doctors of his time. He attended the College of New Jersey (now known as Princeton University) and served as a surgeon during the Revolutionary War. He had been a delegate to the Continental Congress (from Pennsylvania) and one of the signers of the Declaration of Independence.

He and Adams shared the same views on several issues, so Adams would write to him about many things. Sometimes it was about politics; other times it was about philosophy, science, books, family matters, or personal feelings. The correspondence with Rush seemed to give Adams a new energy and excitement, and he looked forward to every new letter from his old friend. Strangely, though, the two men never actually saw each other again.

TRAGIC LOSSES

One of the worst years of Adams's life was 1813. In spite of the happiness of living in his quiet little town, surrounded by books and keeping busy with letter

A letter written by John Adams to Benjamin Rush in 1812

writing, he suffered two losses that would leave him heartbroken. First, his dear friend Benjamin Rush died in April. Rush was only sixty-seven at the time, and Adams had written to him the day before, unaware that he was even ill. And then in August, a second death came, this one even harder to accept—his daughter, Nabby, died after a long battle with breast cancer. She was only forty-nine and had been relatively healthy for most of her life. Adams and his wife were so crushed by the loss that they rarely left their home for the next month.

In the fall of 1818 Abigail was struck with an illness known as typhoid fever. There were no antibiotics at that time, and typhoid killed thousands. Abigail had actually survived a similar illness once before, but this time she was in her midseventies. Adams stayed by her side day and night. Abigail told him she was sure she was going to die. She did so on October 28, and her funeral was held a few days later. They had been together as husband and wife for more than fifty years.

PRESIDENT ADAMS—AGAIN

Following Abigail's death, John Adams, now alone and approaching ninety, kept himself busy with his books and his letters. He and Thomas Jefferson continued writing about everything from current political issues to the miseries of growing older.

Meanwhile, President James Monroe was finishing up his term in office, and a new president was needed. John Quincy Adams was one of four candidates in the election of 1824— and of the other three, only Andrew Jackson, a general and hero from the War of 1812, had a real chance of beating him. In the end the election was too close to call, so the House of Representatives had to make the deciding vote, given the presidency to Adams.

It was one of the proudest moments of John Adams's life— although he did say a few weeks earlier, "No man who ever held the office of President would congratulate a friend on obtaining it." He could not help but remember his own struggles in the job, and he made a point, no doubt, of warning his son that it wouldn't be easy.

Adams Says Good-Bye

After his son's election to the presidency, John Adams's health began to fail. By 1826 he and Jefferson were still writing letters to each other, but not as often. The two old friends were both tired, both ill, and both moving closer to death. Jefferson sent his grandson, Thomas Jefferson Randolph, to visit with Adams in April, and Adams wrote later that month to thank Jefferson for sending him. It was the last note either would write to the other.

By late June, Adams was barely able to move or speak. He had a doctor and a few family members with him at all times. It was thought he might not even

John Adams lived long enough to see the election of his son, John Quincy as president of the United States.

survive into July, but he did. It seemed as though he was determined to live until July 4. Since the year was 1826, that Fourth of July was particularly special—it marked the fiftieth anniversary of the signing of the Declaration of Independence.

John Adams did live to see it. On July 4 he said, "It is a great day. It is a good day." Then, in a whisper later on, he added, "Thomas Jefferson survives." It was a comment on the fact that his old friend had survived him. What Adams didn't know, however, was that Jefferson had died just a few hours earlier.

Shortly after six o'clock that evening, Adams, too, died. And so ended the life of one of the greatest figures in American history.

The second president of the United States, John Adams lived a life dedicated to winning independence for America and committed to the welfare of his beloved countrymen.

TIMELINE

1735
Born October 30 in Braintree, Massachusetts, to John and Susanna Adams

1751–1755
Attends Harvard College

1756–1758
Studies law under the guidance of Worcester attorney James Putnam

1759
Passes bar exam and practices law

1764
Marries Abigail Smith

1774
Attends the First Continental Congress

1775–1781
Attends the Second Continental Congress

1730

1776
Helps draft the Declaration of Independence

1780–1788
Lives in Europe as an American minister

1789
Elected as vice president of the United States with President George Washington

1792
Reelected as vice president of the United States

1796
Wins presidential election against Thomas Jefferson

1800
Loses bid for a second term as president to Thomas Jefferson

1826
Dies at home on July 4

1830

GLOSSARY

Alien and Sedition Acts set of four laws drawn up by the Federalist-controlled Congress that gave the president the power to remove or imprison dangerous aliens from the United States and also to punish any citizens who spoke out against the U.S. government

aquit to be judged not guilty and set free

Bill of Rights first ten amendments to the U.S. Constitution, which define the civil rights of all American citizens

Congress (of the United States) governmental body whose job it is to discuss and create new laws and, on occasion, adjust existing laws

Constitution (of the United States) set of laws, rights, and privileges created at the Constitutional Convention of 1787 and used to build the foundation of the American governmental system; outlines the powers (and limitations of powers) of the government as well as the rights of the people

deacon Protestant who assists a minister with various duties

delegate person who represents others

Democratic-Republican Party (first called the Republican Party) one of the first two formal political parties in the United States, which supported the belief that the bulk of political power should be in the hands of the people or, at the very least, the state governments rather than the federal government

deport to expel from a country

Federalist Party one of the first two formal political parties in the United States, which supported the belief that the bulk of political power should be in the hands of the federal government

French Revolution (1789–1799) change in political and governmental power in France achieved through several bloody battles between the French monarchy and the people

Republican Party *See* Democratic-Republican Party

Stamp Act tax levied on the American colonists in 1765 by the British government in an attempt to recover some of the costs of the French and Indian War

Townshend Acts taxes that were instituted to allow the British government to collect money from the American colonists on imported household and business items, such as glass, paint, paper, and tea

Further Information

Books

Bobrick, Benson. *Fight for Freedom: The American Revolutionary War*. New York: Atheneum Books, 2004.

Fremont-Barnes, Gregory and Richard A. Ryerson. *American Revolutionary War: A Student Encyclopedia*. Santa Barbara, CA: ABC-CLIO, 2007.

Kent, Zachary. *John Adams: Creating a Nation*. Berkeley Heights, NJ: Enslow Publishers, 2004.

Web Sites

Archiving Early America
http://www.earlyamerica.com/
Links, games, and lots of information about early America, particularly the 1700s.

The White House
http://www.whitehouse.gov/history/presidents/ja2.html
A brief biography of Adam's life, with links.

Biography of John Adams
http://www.let.rug.nl/usa/P/ja2/about/bio/adamsxx.htm
A longer biography of Adam's life, with links.

The American Revolution

http://www.kidinfo.com/American_History/American_
Revolution.html
Plenty of solid information about the American Revolution, plus hundreds of links to other sites.

Massachusetts Historical Society

http://www.masshist.org/welcome/
A site full of information about the Adams family.

BIBLIOGRAPHY

Carlisle, Rodney P. *One Day in History: July 4, 1776*. New York: Collins, 2006.

Diggins, John Patrick. *John Adams*. New York: Times Books, 2003.

Ferling, John E. *Adams vs. Jefferson: The Tumultuous Election of 1800*. New York: Oxford University Press, 2004.

Grant, James. *John Adams: Party of One*. New York: Farrar, Straus and Giroux, 2005.

McCullough, David. *1776*. New York: Simon & Schuster, 2005.

———. *John Adams*. New York: Simon & Schuster, 2001.

Staloff, Darren. *Hamilton, Adams, Jefferson: The Politics of Enlightenment and the American Founding*. New York: Hill and Wang, 2005.

Vidal, Gore. *Inventing a Nation: Washington, Adams, Jefferson*. New Haven, CT: Yale University Press, 2003.

INDEX

Pages in **boldface** are illustrations.

ABOUT THE AUTHOR

Wil Mara is the author of more than eighty books, many of which are reference titles for young readers. Information about his work can be found at www.wilmara.com.

4/12 (9)